MW01283713

*10 Powerful Networking
Secrets of Influential People*

Library of Congress

ISBN: 978-1-5005263-5-1

Other Books by Carl E. Reid

10 Powerful Networking Tips Using Business Cards - Global Extended Edition

101 Ways To Be Fearless At Work

Foreword author in the book
Win the Race for 21st Century Jobs
by Rod Colón.

*** Please Write a Review of This Book at www.Amazon.com ***

Thank you SO MUCH for taking time out of your busy schedule to write a review of this book. Your review is an important contribution to helping SAVVY INTRAPRENUER improve the global world around us, one professional at a time. Good or bad, your feedback helps improve the quality of information shared.

This book is dedicated to . . .

My father, Joseph A. Reid, who never knew a stranger, took me on trips to different countries and taught me valuable networking and public speaking skills.

My mother, Mercedes V. Reid, who taught me etiquette and always reminded me "There is never an excuse for bad manners".

My charming wife and business partner, **Phyllis M. Shelton** for her patience, understanding and encouragement. As my business partner for 20 years, I'm proud to say Phyllis is CEO and founder of iPower Global Solutions, a very successful event production company and well respected political consultant.

My siblings, Laura, Lyle, Bruce and Noel who love and supported me throughout the years, despite my imperfections.

All my extended family and people in my international global network, who have contributed a kind word, listened to my ideas or pinged me via email, phone or text message to just say "Hey".

Table of Contents

What is a Savvy Intrapreneur?

Since my company **SAVVY INTRAPRENEUR** is the publisher of my books and blogs, the benefits of being a "**Savvy Intrapreneur**" is provided. First, let's answer the question "What is an Intrapreneur?"

Gifford Pinchot coined the word "**Intrapreneur**" in the 1970's. An Intrapreneur thinks like an entrepreneur seeking out opportunities, which benefit the corporation. It was a new way of thinking, in making companies more productive and profitable. IBM was one of the 1st companies to execute the Intrapreneur approach, when it spun off a separate company as its personal computer division, in the early 1980's. The entire leadership of the new company was made up entirely of Intrapreneurs. Risk taking, visionary employees who thought like entrepreneurs.

A Savvy Intrapreneur takes a good idea and makes it better.

A Savvy Intrapreneur steps out of the comfort zone of corporate security, to insure s/he creates additional income which at least matches their take home pay. An Intrapreneur works overtime helping to run someone else's business, for the company's future. A Savvy Intrapreneur runs themselves like a profitable business putting in 1 hour a day of overtime for their own financial future.

Developing a career while maintaining position at work requires staying focused as a Savvy Intrapreneur. This takes courage.

Are you ready? Then step out. Dare to make yourself "fireproof" at work.

Foreword by Julio Barreto

As society has evolved technological advances have made it easier to communicate with each other in real time. In taking advantage of how instantly we can connect with each, there is a subtly to interpersonal communication that is diminishing. In your personal and professional life, interacting with people is still critical to establishing fruitful, enriching relationships and successful marriage.

In the professional arena, who you know can be more important than what you know when selling a new product, an idea or seeking employment. The "10 Powerful Networking Secrets of Influential People" offers you, the reader, with quick, easy tips to communicate more effectively with people you meet. Carl E. Reid offers solutions to reaching out to people you associate with – family, friends, clients, associates, partners, etc. - in a way which can make each individual feel special. After all, isn't that the way we all want to feel? Special!

Julio Barreto has 30 years of experience as a successful entrepreneur. Mr. Barreto is a professional speaker and author and seasoned policy expert on local and national issues. Julio is Owner of a very successful global Ecommerce company, Barreto & Associates.

Connect with Julio . . .
www.BarretoAssociates.com
Tel: 240-381-6311
Email: JBarretojr@verizon.net
Facebook.com/juliobarreto57
Linkedin.com/pub/Julio-Barreto/1/475/324

Introduction - You Are a Person of Influence

Being a "person of influence", "change maker" or "rainmaker" are all interchangeable words.

How do you get 300 people to each drop $250,000 for a space flight reservation, which was accomplished by Sir **Richard Branson's** Virgin Galactic?

How does **Barack Obama**, a relatively unknown senator become the 44th President of the United States?

How does **David Geffen** go from working in the mailroom to becoming one of the founders of DreamWorks?

How does **Rod Colón** turn a one day temporary assignment at JP Morgan Chase into being on staff for 13 years? How does Mr. Colón then go on to become one of the top career management experts and "in demand" speaker in the United States?

How does Jibber Jobber, a very successful international global enterprise become founded and headed by CEO, **Jason Alba**, who started the company with no job?

How does the world go into a feverish buying frenzy for a book, when **Oprah Winfrey** mentions it?

How is it that **Keith Ferrazzi** comes from obscurity to be viewed as the Dr. Phil of networking relationship management?

Coming from a major brokerage firm, how does **Suze Orman** become one of Time Magazine's most "Influential People" in 2008. How was Ms. Orman previously designated in Business Week as the top female motivational speaker?

When only we think of influential people the thought of politicians, wealthy people, entertainers and company CEOs immediately comes to mind. We think of a few individuals as having influence. The truth is everyone possesses the power to change things or make an impact without having prestige or wealth. This book will teach you how to carefully cultivate these rainmaker networking skills.

From 0 to Influential

"*Up Through the Mailroom*"
by Martin Lieberman points out a
mail room clerk or a temporary
worker can exert as much influence
as the company CEO. Michael
Ovitz, Barry Diller, and David

Geffen (one of the founders of Dreamworks) all began their careers in the mailroom of the William Morris agency. I also know this from personal experience. I jump started a very successful 33+ year career in information technology (IT) by working as a temporary mailroom clerk.

Any person who leverages their position, is said to be influential. When someone facilitates a situation that produces a change or particular outcome, that change maker accomplishes those results through with a **focus on developing personal relationships for life**. This is a dedicated lifetime effort to achieve the distinction of being that person of influence, through your network of associations. You must be willing to go beyond the basics of networking.

There are many articles that deal with foundation skills of networking like "*10 Powerful Networking Tips Using Business Cards*". To reach that rare distinction in being recognized as a person of influence, advanced networking skills must be developed.

In the mid 1990's telephone companies were charging per minute rates. My wife was livid every time I paid a $700 to $800 monthly telephone bill. After a couple of years she once commented "you're always calling people, but very few call you. When they call, they usually want something". The jaw dropping look on her face was priceless when I responded with "honey, if anything ever happens to me you can call anyone in my contact database and they will help you, without hesitation". I never again heard another word from my wife about the telephone bill. Thank goodness for flat rate telephone billing these days, as I continue to reach out and touch people.

The powerful networking secrets covered in this book are habits to slowly implement. Going beyond basic networking approaches, each of these advanced networking techniques requires a bit more work to achieve results that <u>will better position you as a person of influence</u>.

1. Elevate Your Network

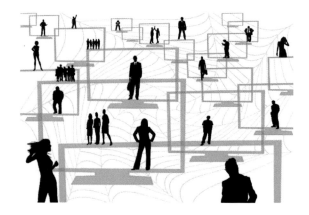

Start to develop 5 star relationships within your network. You can have many people in your network. Which person(s) can you call, right now, who would not hesitate to help you. A free tool called Jibber Jobber has a feature that facilitates this process. To the untrained eye this feature appears innocuous. It provides a 1 to 5 star ranking system for each contact.

When used properly it elevates a person's network, while improving relationship skills that achieve powerful outcomes. You become a person of influence by continuously staying in touch with people, without asking for anything. You connect with proven people of influence, who reciprocate by touching base with you regularly.

Proper use of the Jibber Jobber contact ranking feature involves slowly upgrading the star level for each person. It's up to you to decide how you want to rank your contacts. For me it's a combination of the longevity of me staying in touch and how the person responds in kind. When these 2 criteria are met [or not] my 5 star contact rankings are adjusted accordingly.

The goal is to have 200 five star contacts. These are the top people relationships in your network.

Be patient. 5 star contacts take time to cultivate. Over time they become those few persons of influence that you can rely on, because they know they can rely on you for assistance. This only occurs by being disciplined in consistently reaching out to 5 star contacts. Below are smart ways to stay in touch, while maximizing your most valuable commodity called "time".

Do you have a system for managing your network contacts?
Please share with **Email to**
IGetSmart@SavvyIntrapreneur.com
You get credit in the next book update, if published.

2. Nourish Your Network

Share information related to each contact's interests. You have a business associate that collects stamps. Keep an eye out for stamp collecting articles to send that person. When opportunities or relative networking events come into your email inbox, share them with your network.

Call or ping (email, text message etc.) 1 to 2 persons in your network each day.

Reconnect and warm up old contacts by sharing articles of interest to that <u>specific person</u>, free tools like the NY Times **Deal Book** app, **JibberJobber.com** or **Smart Radar** or free associations with warm trusted global networks, like **Empowering Today's Professionals**.

Making deposits into the **good will bank** always <u>places you in a position of influence</u>. People are more receptive to being contacted when you **show an interest** in them. Think of creative ways to keep your name in front of people all the time.

How do you nourish your network? Email your tips.
IGetSmart@SavvyIntrapreneur.com
You get credit in the next book update, if published.

3. High Tech High Touch

Email

Let people know what's happening in your professional life. Send out reprints of articles along with a quick note. One of the easiest ways of doing this is by setting up a mailing list. The small investment in time will pay huge dividends.

Voicemail

Your outgoing message and messages you leave can be powerful marketing and networking tools. **Get voice mail tips** on the SavvyIntrapreneur.com web site

blog.
http://www.savvyintrapreneur.com/2
005/12/voice-mail-etiquette-make-it-
memorable.html

Make Email Your Silent Sales Tool

Never assume friends or associates have your contact information readily available. Phones break, computers crash and little black books get lost and life has a nasty habit of quickly distracting people in a New York City minute.

The easier you make it for anyone to get in touch with you, the faster they will contact you. When you COMPOSE, REPLY or FORWARD it, have contact information in your email signature.

More email tips . . .
http://itechspeak.blogspot.com/2010/
11/how-to-get-people-to-ignore-
your-emails.html

Creating a mailing list of people in your trusted network.

To stay in compliance with the U.S. Canned Spam Act of 2003, consider using a list server. This technology works much better than most newsletter list services.

A "listserv" is a distribution group of email addresses that is represented by a single email address. Posting or sending a message to the list single address causes it to be forwarded to all the "subscriber" addresses on the distribution list.

The main difference between a listserv and an email system is the way email is delivered to each subscriber. If 200 subscribers on your 700 email distribution list have AOL email accounts, the listserv **delivers to each person individually, one at a time** to the

25

AOL email system. When you send email through your personal email system, all 200 AOL emails are sent, enmasse, all at one time. This is the trip wire for AOL and all other email providers to flag legitimate, friendly email as spam or bulk commercial email.

These days sending email to more than 10-15 email addresses in the same mailing, may be considered spam. A list server best minimizes spam related issues, while automatically allowing list subscribers to opt IN and OUT.

Below are some suggested cost effective resources for managing mailing lists, which I use and recommend to clients. Personal or company organization branding is optional.

- ➢ **www.ElectricEmbers.coop Groups -**
  Hat tip to **Benjamin**, **Brent**, and **Adam** for their excellence in service at Electric Embers, celebrating 10+ years of community listserv service. Tell them Carl E. Reid referred you.

- ➢ **www.Aweber.com**

- ➢ **LSoft.com**

What mailing list do you use?
Send **Email to**
IGetSmart@SavvyIntrapreneur.com
You get credit in the next book update, if published.

4. Create Your Own Business Card

Working as an employee at a company should not prevent you from having a business card. If your company provides you with business cards, that's great. If not, invest in making your own business cards.

Just pay for shipping and you can get free business cards at **VistaPrint.com**. Read ***10 Powerful Networking Tips Using Business Cards Global Extended Edition*** to begin your campaign of influencing people with your business cards.

5. Schedule Relationship Development

    In addition to using LinkedIn, consider using true client / contact relationship management software, like **FreeCRM.com** or **Nimble.com**. These cloud based programs fine tune the tracking of your interactions with people. **Evernote Hello** emails your contact information within minutes of a first time meeting.

Developed by author and speaker, Harvey Mackay, I highly recommend incorporating the **Mackay 66**. This powerful tool is essential for developing 5 star contacts. Grab your free copy **http://www.harveymackay.com/tools/mackay-66**

When I have a conversation with someone, I write notes in their electronic contact card. The Mackay 66 allows me to have a superior memory the next time I speak with each person. I reference personal tidbits mentioned previously. (i.e. did your son pass that test, did your meeting go well, did your anniversary dinner go well etc.). Entering the date I last spoke to someone produces a wonderful result. Entering the date of a conversation allows me to keep up people I have not talked to in 60, 90, 120 days etc.. Now I can catch up with a quite few people each week.

Schedule personal meetings over breakfast, lunch, dinner or cup of coffee. There is no substitute for personal interaction. If an associate is coming to your local area, it's always nice to see a friendly face. So be disciplined about scheduling regular meet ups throughout the month.

LinkedIn has an awesome tool for pinging contacts. Click on the ***Connections*** menu option. LinkedIn will provide you with connection activity, like starting a new job, birthday, job anniversary and recent geographical move. Using this excellent pinging tool allows me to perform 2-5 minutes of daily connection engagement. Just like a commercial, you keep your face in front of people, start conversations and reconnect with people in your network. Your influence increases exponentially, as you make these daily rounds with different people.

6. Library of Power Networking Champions

These are recommended books that helped me develop solid personal and business relationships, keeping me well fed on my journey called success. May these suggested readings make your networking travels even more rewarding.

Swim With Sharks Without Being Eaten Alive by Harvey MacKay

Win The Race For 21st Century Jobs by Rod Colón

Little Black Book of Connections by Jeffrey Gitomer

How to Win Friends and Influence People by Dale Carnegie

How to Really Use LinkedIn by Jan Vermeiren

Skill with People by Les Giblin

Networking Magic by Rick Frishman & Jill Lublin

Never East Alone by Keith Ferrazzi and Tahl Raz

The Power of Approachability by Scott Ginsberg

Turn Small Talk into Big Deals by Don Gabor

I'm On LinkedIn. Now What? by Jason Alba

Endless Referrals by Bob Burg

What books have you read that have increased your networking influence? Your suggestion will be consider for the next revision of this book. Yes, you get credit too, if it is printed.

Send your book suggestion to IGetSmart@SavvyIntrapreneur.com

7. How to Win an Argument

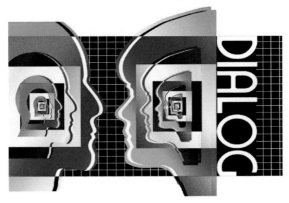

I have learned that any person who is perceived as the best in their field, deftly combines core skills with well honed interpersonal skills. It takes a finite amount of time to achieve an education in developing a core skill foundation in a chosen career (i.e. 2-4 years of college or a business school). It takes a lifetime to develop good interpersonal skills. Why? Each interaction with a person is unique and different.

I have recently been revisiting *How to Win Friends and Influence*

People by Dale Carnegie. I often refer to this book as my human relations reference manual.

Below is a paraphrased excerpt from one of my favorite chapters; *You Can't Win an Argument*.

> ➢ Be open to disagreement.

> ➢ Check your temper.

> ➢ Listen for opportunity.

> ➢ Stay open for common areas to agree.

> ➢ Make a commitment to carefully think over the other person's ideas.

> ➢ The only way to get the best of an argument is to do everything in your power to totally avoid it.

8. Edification: The Super Glue of Power Networkers

In "***The Serving Leader***"
authors Ken Jennings and John
Stahl-Wert provide 2 key leadership

responsibilities. Leaders teach others the knowledge, skills and strategies they need to succeed. Leaders also work hard to get obstacles out of the way of others so they can make progress.

Edification is a powerful technique for helping others develop confidence skills, while removing obstacles created by lack of confidence. Very few organizations promote the encouraging art of edification. If you cross paths with an opportunity **to join a team of people who promote, teach and live edification** as part of their training support, <u>do not hesitate</u> embracing this life changing way of building confidence. Power networkers understand how to leverage edification for developing powerful trusted relationships.

Webster defines edification as "the act of edifying, or the state of being edified; a building up, especially in a moral or spiritual sense; moral, intellectual, or spiritual improvement; instruction".

Edification can be learned by anyone in just a few minutes. It does take practice intertwining edification into daily life. It immediately builds confidence for the person being edified and the person [leader] doing the edification.

In networking terms, edifying another person shines a 10,000 watt spotlight on him/her, which reflects doubly back on you. People will naturally want to be around you when you edify others.

Edifying others is the glue for making people stick with you and be associated with anything you are involved in. Edification empowers you to create your own following. When you tell your network "I'm going to be at this event, fund raiser, conference, etc.", people willingly make it their business to be there.

Here are some suggested approaches successful networking leaders use to instill confidence and develop rock solid trusted networks, through edification:

RING LEADER

So you planned and coordinated an event. Always introduce the speaker so a connection is made with the audience. While presenting the speaker's bio, speak from the heart about your association.

Even a known returning speaker should be edified, through the introduction. This sets the stage for engaging attendees to listen more closely to the speaker.

DAISEY CHAIN

This is one of my favorite edification approaches. It creates a chain reaction of networking self empowerment. If a few people have put an event together, ask someone on the team to introduce another team member who knows either the speaker or most of the attendees. Then have that person introduce the speaker. This allows 2 team members to edify each other, just in case the speaker knows nothing about edification. This makes a powerful impression on attendees. Making introductions is an excellent way to practice public speaking skills, especially for new team members.

TAG TEAM

1. You are going to an event with a friend. Give each friend a few of your business cards. As you meet people edify the other person by talking up each other's skills or business. Then give your friend's

business card to the person you just met.

2. Let's say 2 people are talking at an event. You know one of them and s/he introduces you. Edify your friend by highlighting their skills, business or good qualities.

FAMILY TIES

Nothing improves family relationships better than edification.

Edify Your Parents

As my dad told me, I have shared with my children and grand children. No matter where you travel in this world your actions represent and are a reflection of your parents. So edify your parents by acting in a manner towards other people, which shines a bright, positive spotlight on your parents. Alive or deceased, make your parents proud. Only write content (i.e. email) your mother would be proud to read.

Edify Your Children

This builds better relationships between child and parent, while instilling confidence in children, tweens and teenagers. Some examples . . .This is my daughter / son . . . s/he is a wiz at math - on the football team - is studying hard for the SAT - is a terrific person . . .

Edify Your Spouse

Elevate your spouse with augmented introductions. Some examples . . . This is my wife and business partner - This is my husband who is a top notch expert in the technology field - This is my life partner who is very successful in the health care industry . . .

Always edify your spouse in front of your children, by supporting each other's decisions. Settle child rearing issues with your spouse in private.

Saying "thank you", "please" and "can you do me a favor" are also forms of edifying family members. It develops respect and trust, while getting family members to more willingly accomplish tasks.

PRIVATE SESSIONS

Use one on one personal conversations to encourage and support a friend, by focusing on their strengths. Although it may be hard, even highlighting good qualities with a difficult co-worker may help project them to the space where they need to be. Building confidence, through edification, is sometimes all it takes to get a foe on your side of the table.

What networking techniques have you used? Send **Email to** IGetSmart@SavvyIntrapreneur.com
You get credit in the next book update, if published.

9. Power Broker Email Connections

Making an introduction by providing an associate with just an email address or telephone number is the mark of amateur networking. This provides a cold connection. Position yourself as a power broker by personally connecting 2 people. A much warmer connection is established, when you copy both people using email.

Edify each person to give reasons why they should connect. In the email talk up your personal association with each person. For example, "Joanne is a trusted friend and business associate . . . we worked previously at . . . s/he possesses business savvy / sold technical skills that helped me / company XYZ achieve . . .".

10. Rainmaker 101

```
s t r a t e g y
s u c c e s s
p r o f i t
s a l e s
c r e a t i v i t y
b u s i n e s s
o r g a n i z a t i o n
n e t w o r k i n g
g l o b a l
w o r l d w i d e
t r a d e
i m p o r t
e x p o r t
i n t e r n a t i o n a l
```

Enter the rainmaker, the
subject of movies and mythology,
part human-part god.

The truth is anyone has the potential be a rainmaker. It takes a solution oriented positive attitude, highly developed interpersonal skills, trained senses to constantly spot opportunities and most importantly, courage in taking risks.

Intrapreneurs and entrepreneurs are rainmakers in training. It's a work in progress to be a consistent rainmaker. S/He is someone people are attracted to with a willingness to work collaboratively on projects.

Within organizations certain departments are looked upon as rainmakers in their ability to sustain or increase a company's financial growth. It could be the sales force in an insurance company. In the banking arena, the trading floor is the prized group. The fund raising department in a non-profit organization walks on water.

Rainmakers can also be individual people who develop business for themselves or their company. Being a rainmaker is not necessarily related to just finances. Yes, they are great business developers when placed in that role. But, rainmakers are also people who rise to become leaders and affect change in themselves and others. They strive for balanced personal and career lives. Rainmakers are successes in their field, mentors, role models, and magnets for people attracted to excellence. . .

The hallowed title of rainmaker is not always bestowed upon the swiftest, fastest, smartest or toughest. A person can establish their self as that "go to" person by looking for opportunities to solve problems. Rainmakers solidify their position by leveraging their network, for any problem they cannot solve.

No person is the be all and end all, unless they increase their sphere of influence. Developing an ever expanding network, ensures continuous sources for acquiring resources to assist in solving problems. The learned ability to solve problems, always insures several sources of continuous income.

2 hallmarks of a rainmaker is 1) be willing to personally connect someone who needs something with a person who has something and 2)work towards developing relationships for life.

BONUS: Cool Tools for Monitoring Social Media Influence

www.Klout.com, Google Alerts www.google.com/alerts and **www.NutShellMail.com** by Constant Contact are "must have" tools to monitor your influence in the Internet community. As Bob Burg mentions in his book "**Endless Referrals**", people like to do business with persons they **know**, **like** and **trust**. These 3 variables contribute to "influence". How do you verify and adjust how your social media presence adds value to people? Which friends, business associates, clients or potential customers like, comment or share your postings.

What's Your Klout Score?

Klout.com uses a reasonably fair scoring system that represents your overall social media influence. The algorithms behind the **Klout.com** score considers 400 variables on multiple social networks, beyond your followers and friends on LinkedIn, Facebook or Twitter. **Klout.com** lets you know who is engaged with your content and who is sharing what you contribute with their network.

Use **Klout.com** to receive solid intelligence on how your influence is perceived by others. Then make adjustments on your different social media platforms.

Google Alerts for Reputation Monitoring

If you want eyes and ears in the back of your head to know who's talking about you, consider **Google Alerts** as your new best friend. Maybe you're old enough to remember clipping services. Prior to the Internet, companies engage a clipping service to cut out and snail mail (USPS) all company related stories in back to the company. This allowed companies to keep their finger on the pulse of what was being said, good or bad, about that company.

Founder of **Social Media DIY Workshop** and social media expert, **Charlene Kingston** clearly explains how to do ***Reputation Management with Google Alerts*** at **http://socialmediadiyworkshop.co m/2009/12/reputation-management-with-google-alerts** - Hat tip to Charlene's web site SocialMediaDIYWorkshop.com for being an excellent resource to develop networking influence using various social media platforms.

Nutshell Mail is Your Trusted Facebook Consigliere

NutShellMail.com is Google Alerts for your Facebook business page. It is designed to email you whenever posts or comments are made, by other people, on your Facebook Business or Personal page.

Managing your influence (aka - doing damage control) is a breeze when you are "in the know" and can quickly delete undesirable posts or comments from your Facebook business / personal page. You can also monitor the influence of any competitor's Facebook business page.

Last Thoughts . . .

Becoming a person of influence requires developing advanced networking skills. It will require extra time and effort, but the dividends are huge for expanding your sphere of influence.

Ongoing development of relationships positions you to ask for help from others. Being able to leverage your influence with your network, to help others, makes you the rainmaker people will constantly seek out.

About Author: Carl E. Reid

With corporate travels from the mail room to the board room, Carl E. Reid knows what it takes to be successful. An early adopter of Intrapreneur career management, Carl has over 46 years of business experience, including 32 years as a technology expert, 22 years as a business career coach and 25 years as a successful entrepreneur. Carl has been a professional blogger and social media strategist since 2004. In addition to being a sought after speaker and published author, Mr. Reid has coached and inspired hundreds of people to land jobs and start successful businesses. Carl is Executive Director for Empowering Today's Professionals, a 501(c)3 career management educational non-profit.

Working with over 50 companies in diverse industries during a 46 year business career, some of Carl's clients include IBM(technology consulting), JP Morgan Chase (global banking), OXYGEN (TV/media), Sotheby's (auction), New York City Health & Hospitals, Shearman & Sterling (legal), McGraw Hill (publishing), Moët Hennessy - LVMH, Insurance Services Office.

According to Google, Carl's article *10 Powerful Networking Tips Using*

Business Cards has been published on over 50,000 web sites and blogs.

CONNECT with Carl . . .
www.CarlEReid.com

Twitter.com/CarlEReid

Facebook.com/SavvyIntrapreneur

Linkedin.com/in/CarlEReid

Get FREE updates via Email or RSS reader at **Library of Congress Recognized** Blog
www.SavvyIntrapreneur.com
Twitter.com/Intrapreneur

Tel: 201-222-5390

Email:
IGetSmart@SavvyIntrapreneur.com

****

PLEASE WRITE A REVIEW OF THIS BOOK ON AMAZON.COM

Made in the USA
Lexington, KY
19 September 2016